For A
Judy
on
her
birthday
March 26
2003 (2023)

Love
Laura

sparks

Sparks

Laura Chester

Photographs by Donna DeMari

THE FIGURES
2002

Some of these prose poems first appeared in:
Proud & Ashamed, Christopher's Books, 1978
Lupus Novice, Station Hill Press, 1987, 2000
Free Rein, Burning Deck, 1988
In the Zone, Black Sparrow Press, 1988
All in All, Quale Press, 2000
Wake Up Heavy, edited by Mark Begley
Birch Lane, Vol. 1, No. 2, edited by Bruce Barone
The World, edited by Lewis Warsh

The quote, "*Entering into the fragrant twilight ...*"
was taken from Hannah Green's book, *Little Saint*,
Random House, © 2000 by the estate of Hannah Green

The Figures, 5 Castle Hill, Great Barrington, MA 01230
Distributed by SPD, 1341 7th Street, Berkeley, CA 94710-1403
Typeset by Chad Odefey
www.laurachester.com
word@laurachester.com

ISBN: 1-930589-13-1

for George & Laura

As gold in the furnace, he has proved them,
  And as sacrificial offerings he took them to himself.
In the time of their visitation they shall shine
  And dart about as sparks amongst the stubble.

— *The Book of Wisdom*

Our vanity, our passions, our spirit of imitation, our abstract intelligence, our habits have long been at work, and it is the task of art to undo this work of theirs, making us travel back in the direction from which we have come to the depth where what has really existed lies unknown within us.

— *Marcel Proust*

part one

THE SPARK SO quickly becomes the fire becomes you. Your face is shining with the light all around, like a mane. Aura, luster, a polished egg. Eager and willing to bend the saplings, weigh them down, to cradle the candle flame within. Get out a match. The tent of kindling safe in its bunk of sand and stone. Or is it just *this* that excites us, leads us on, illicit touch. The torch is lit– it shines in the iris. Warm beeswax and sherry wine. What draws us here to our private shed, to our lair in the woods– (*is chocolate*.

HOMEMADE STRUCTURES built in the heart of *knock-on-wood*. All absorbed til even now inside this book of yours. A scratching place to make your marks, *wordsincode*, cuneiform, moonbeam guardian of secret stuff. Open the lid and out spring the nasties, incandescent, slippering-slidey through the fingers. Hide me, hurry– Get the folded map with penciled X which surely marks The Spot. Here our treasure lies hidden, stashed away. Dug up, cracked open. Spilling its jewels. Pretend so hard you forget to go home. Dig and dig for the rest of your life– (*trying to remember.*

LITTLE LUSTER, shine resplendent, gliding over a grassy path to a place of shelter. Rest your head in my nesting lap. *Entering into the fragrant twilight of the fir wood, we feel we are in a holy grove, protected...* Keeper of clarion, twists of glint and colored yarn– golden doves adorn the air. Newborn lambikin's ululation. Behind the heartbone of her tiny shrine, lies a rose kept folded.

NO SIDE WHEELS all-of-a-sudden– I'm *aloft* on my own blue Schwinn with finger ringer and plastic streamers, basket stuffed with red windbreaker. How'd I do it? Steady pedal and single gear, all bright blue but, no bar, cause I'm a girl. On My Own! Don't *think* about it. Not to fall but only pedal, (being held) by almost air or– (*how keep going?*

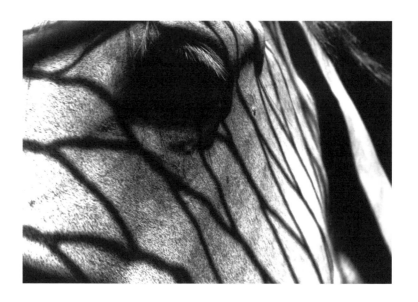

NOW IT IS YOUR TURN– under lock and key, can you? This is my life in yellow diary with brass parts. Broken into. One of the many violations. Thought it was safe in the maple drawer of my bedside table, between four posters. I needed a stool to mount that bed. Up so high there was plenty of space for a monster man with beard and hat, who lay beneath the blue cotton skirt of it, waiting to crush me, to– (*bury my breath*.

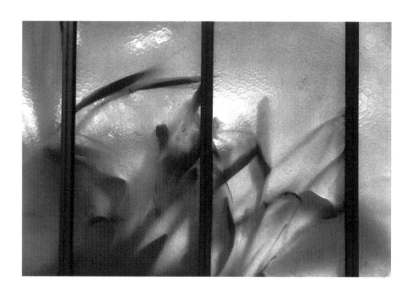

MOTHER OPENS MY secret drawers disguised as columns, where I hide love letters from Weiner Pop-pop. Small compartments, dividing things. This jewelry box of the budding brain. List of best and worst friends. Arranging and pasting, throwing things out. Under my bed where I write what feels like nails through wood, making me suffer my older brother, too hard to imagine through hands and foot. Scoot down under and lie on my back, write on the raft that supports my bed– code of passion and dirty words, initials of current boys beloved, insignia horse face, C-A-M, which stands for– (*cigarettes, alcohol, men.*

SLEEPING DOWN RIVER, floating along, or up on my shoulders to walk the canopy *upside-down-cake*. Hiking up, holding my butt to touch my toes to the bones of the bars that hold the ruffled, dotted swiss covering, (very feminine) which I am not. Pink horse pills for swollen glands, my silk pup with floppy ears, caramel smooth, underarm. Don't want to share with a sleep-talking sister, so take to the attic, which is even worse. I *hear* something! Turn every light on in the house– until it is blazing– "*You were always such a scary,* scary *child.*"

SPRING SQUEAKING rocker in a yellow room
where tissue thin curtains luff back in– lying beneath
the backyard lilacs in a self-made hollow of powdered
earth– burying my nose in the golden collie's sun-
baked mane– sound of the wavelets, scum on the
shore– tiny checks of my uniform– crouched as the
catcher, hit by a bat, above the eye, no-such-thing-as
an accident. Moments of pain. Moments of pleasure.
Stubbed toes and cocoa butter. (But why, I wonder,
do these particulars, we remember?

ONE CAN NOT FORCE IT, only tease, tickle it open.
Boys by the swing set getting a peek. Nobody talks
about how we liked it, even the *thought* of getting a
touch. My neighborhood crush was offering money
to pull down drawers. I was tempted, but Lindsay did
it. Leslie too. In her saggy white cotton little girl
underpants. I lived next-door and dreamed out my
window, touching myself. The two of them down on
the basement carpet. Caught with the twig set. *Red
light Green light.* Her built "bod" soon to explode.
Egg cracked open, slime down shirt. Thinking and
thinking about what I had seen. Slithering hand runs
up her cupcake– pulsing, pushing, all of a sudden, toes
are taut and sparks– (*strewn.*

EVERYONE'S BACKYARD connecting with bushes,
metal gates with squeezable latches, exit holes under
scratch wire fences, cyclone, falling full into boxwood
hedges, making a crush mark, digging a hole, filling it
up with a mystery mixture, scooping it out, poured
onto cement, running down corridors between brick
buildings– we crouch at the end, lining up miniature
colored bottles, empty of alcohol. Then we smoke,
inhale and swear, scratch our arms with a red hot pin.
Three L's leaping– throwing the SPUD ball, kicking the
can, calling out numbers... now– (*you're IT !*

TAKE OVER YOUR OWN life, under the bridge, in
dark garages– I saw something in the twilight memory
of sprinkler summers that blends together with ruffled
chips and peanut butter sandwiches. Towers of Ritz.
Listening for the *two-three-four-clang* dinner bell,
watching the streetlamps. Time to head home to tuna
noodle casserole in birdnest baskets. Crossing the
boundary to The Popcorn Stand on the corner of
Downer, long wax fingers and sexy lips, necklace of
candy on stretch elastic, pastel dots on white strips.
All of this just across the street from St. Paul's
Episcopal, making life difficult, cause– (*dirt sticks.*

REPEATED RITE of round the block ritual, taking my
boxer for his daily double. Over cracks in the laid
cement, slanted parts of the city sidewalk, certain
houses where you held your breath, sections of
smoothness, good for skates. Home of the loved
one– we played 4-square. (I'd *pay* to shovel his walk
or mow.) Mausoleum with the two black devil dogs,
mystery house on the tip of the block, always dark,
gate never open, friendly elders and monster mansions–
Harnishfeger, Tolan, Eschweiler, Hokenson, Esser,
Anderson, Dickenson, Brown. Once my world–
(*now we are gone.*

METAL TRIM AROUND the Formica counter of our 50's kitchen– diamond window in the swinging door where the budgie bird got it, *scars askew*. Breakfast nook where my brother dissected until I swore I would never eat eggs, (including eggplant. There in the middle, on the kitchen floor, an old card table, but a perfect cube. Close to provisions– jelly jar milk and tollhouse cookies hot from the sheet. A wobbly table with slipcover lid made to fit the same dimensions. Crouched in our cottage with painted window and flap-like door, we entered our own world, dropping crumbs on the tiles of the floor. But would we escape the blazing oven, the coaxing come-on, find our way back through our own dark forest of green linoleum?

SECLUDED CORNERS, earthen alcove, secret cupboards and telephone booths, windowseats and slanted bedrooms, to close yourself in, to keep the world out. Our confessional, on princess phones, telling the truth talking one-to-one. Whispered messages, from ear to mouth, til it comes out gossip. Spines of books, announcing love, my latest attachment. Now everyone's talking, everybody knows. Eating your heart out. Spitting up words. Busy and lonely, on the *hurry-to-get-go*, wandering terminals, looking for the next place to– (*row row row.*

HEAVENLY DEEP DOWN undercover, in my sick bed, a propped up tray, painted yellow, side slots for crayons and Casper comics, canned white cherries, a pattern of pits. The eye travels over the same old wallpaper, over and over, the repeated thing– a burst of flowers, almost *Chinois*, spray of white on a pale pink background, taking comfort in the repetition of things– burst of flowers, like the coming of spring, petals swirl in a sudden confetti above my head– THREE drop into the pages of my book– *"I loved her because I was made to love her,"* (as if it were meant to be.

I HIDE MYSELF under the carport, in the salamander basement with its slick cement and huge oil burner, under the peak of a sweltering attic, beneath the portico where the bikes are kept, under the eyes (thank God) of nobody no one. I hide myself with selected friends. Blood sister/brother– we're together in this. Pull up the comforter, pull down the lid. Cover myself with hot tub water, let it out to the perfect level, lathering soap bar between my legs. I watch myself in the steamed-up mirror, wipe a swatch to see my face– *That's who you'll be til forever is over.* Back into bed to find the warm spot. I hide myself behind musty drapes, inside a leaf hole, in a bare bush nest. I hide myself in a bucket of grass in the middle of the hay field– (*the better to find myself.*

THE MANY WONDERS of a drawstring purse, saved
for the sickbed, filled with finds, examining one thing
after another– blue Delft shoe that fits my finger,
thumbnail book for oval portraits, cloisonné pillbox
filled with pearls, a smooth white stone to kiss the
cheeks with, shiny shell in a perfect spiral, magnifying
lens that swivels out of its brass container, a baby blue
enamel thimble, ivory cross with a pinprick peephole,
where you can see an etching of a miraculous statue,
broken antique wristwatch face whose time you can
turn, a wooden turtle made from bark, baby ammonite
from the Atlas Mountains, a bottle of rose oil, pure
essence– (*two tons of petals, one litre of dew.*

WE HAUL WET STONES to make a circle round the Cootie Rock. Here kisses crawl from the crack. Squeezing in through the doghouse door with scatter of straw on wooden floor, we sit cross-legged, blowing the whistle, one by one, then round the ring, touching each other, *finger-to-forehead*, passed hand signal– everyone silent, and still... then– (*RUN!*

UNDER THE CANOE boat bottom roof, inner ribs
and woven seats with wicker holes, shelves to put
things, sticks and stones. Attics, compartments tucked
under stairs. Houses made out of dry leaves, mud,
dribbled through fingers, snow delved into, grooves
of grass, dug out tunnels and rooms of earth, under
porch decks, statuettes dragged in by hand, setting up
soldiers– This is my portion. *That's my side!* Room
divided by a piece of string. Demarcation in the hot
backseat of our stationwagon. Mixture of foodstuffs,
stirred and stirred. Inverted buckets of hand-packed
sand. Backyard playhouse, in no need of decoration.
Absorbed for hours and hours, unseen. But then one
summer they sold it to the neighbors. We peeked in–
it was all dolled up with tiny iron and running water,
fancy china, we had no need for. Our own childhood–
(locked out.

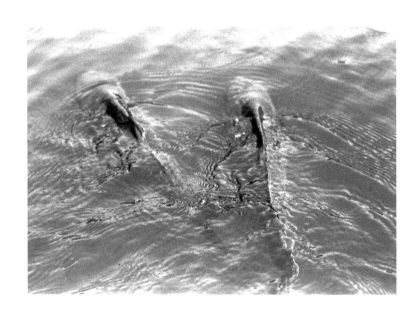

WE WANT RUINS, reckless nature. Want no adults coming near us. Hiding out on some mushy island with red bird berries in a bowl to squish. Secret consumables, scent of cigarettes, blowing smoke through strips of cloth to show the blotch stain of tobacco. We want to do what we aren't supposed to, running around in flannel pajamas, lost boy/girls in underearth caverns. Bursting back into safety and light, in search of my midday tomato sandwich. Once I am fed– (*I am like run off.*

GO, FOR THE TREES are hiding somebody– RUN, *quick* faster than anyone– down to the cottage with its yellow bulb where the mosquitoes gather in a kind of mist. When it is bedtime, June bugs crawl over the screens looking for holes, tactile, clinging. Canvas rolls down as the rain sweeps towards us– *leaping* from bed and back to bed– my brother and I, over "Spit Sea," while Mother rests on her green divan paging through magazines, dreaming of summers anywhere elsewhere, Latin men. Her legs are smooth. Her legs are tan. Toenails painted a shocking pink color in rubber flip-flops. She doesn't know of the dangers right here on the way from the Big House– I run so hard I don't even feel the rough cement and hickory shells, broken open, past tall dark shadows, lurking, leering– (*thank God I am fast.*

EATING OUT THE INSIDES of a roll, blowing bubbles to a froth of milk, piling up a mound of mashers, showing food, peeling plastic from a slice of cheese, little mouse marks all around it. TV dinners, airport food. A bite for every horse I know. Deadly maraschino cherry. Nibbling grahams, breaking saltines carefully on perforations. Dagwood sandwich, stuffing grapes. Find the white dot fluff surprise inside a chocolate Hostess cupcake, squiggle line along the top. Hard rock candy on a string. For these sweet things, *we do sing!* Airplane bites sail through the air– while children starve, in China, elsewhere. Can't we send leftovers there? All those children, have them over? If they're hungry, and we are fed– (*how do I lay me down to bed.*

PEG EATS PAINT while I chew chalk, nip the pink
geranium buds on the way to chapel, chomp on pencils,
Juicy Fruit, five sticks at least, or bland white Beeman's,
sexy feeling in my mouth, guzzling Squirt & Orange
Crush, consuming Milk Duds in the movies, all
crammed in, suicide sundae. Surprise myself and steal
a pacifier from the drugstore. Teensie works her
thumb so hard it sticks her teeth out. We make fun–
"Spider, Blimp, and Olive Oyl." When Peg brings
chocolate-covered ants to Mrs. Anderson's third grade
class, we watch her eat one, *munch munch*, and call
Peg, "BLOCK."

SINGLE HAIRS APPEARING stealthy. Are we poor or are we wealthy? Hip bones jut and butt sticks out. Have you ever seen such calves? Workhorse legs for kicking brothers. Chipper of the floppy ears, flatulence on blue shag carpet, while Tony steals a liquor bottle, holding it behind his back when Mom and Dad come back from somewhere. No one tells him– *Put it back.* That boozy closet makes me nauseous, all those sick smells clashed together. Puddle barf placed on the rug. Hide the red fart fanny cushion to use on Miss Filtration Plant. Laugh so hard we all go spastic. Someone cut one! Blame the boxer. Plastic turd tossed in the dumpster. Blow the horn beneath the bridge near Oscar Meyer's Pig 'n Whistle. HEY, let's stop at Kit's Custard– (*vanilla's not a color, right?*

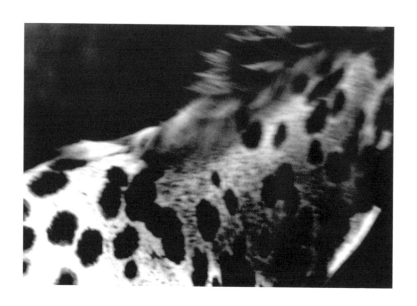

UP THE DIRT HILL we become horses– all girls–
crazed creatures. Riding along then– wildly racing up
the dirt mound– King of the Hill, not queen we go–
down *Down* the slope of the hard-packed, throwing
manes and kicking out. Horse legs bracing. "Too bad
you didn't inherit your mother's." *Uh-oh.* I stormed
the hill and Reigned Supreme. Stomped my loafer
hoof– (and *screamed!*

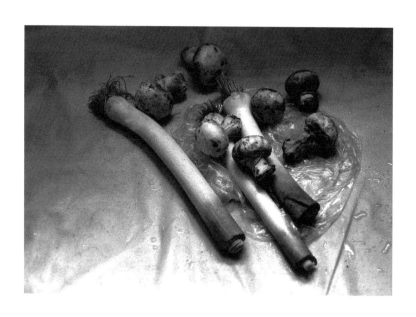

LIFT THE LID, a plain white shoebox, lined with
clippings. Place him very softly in, with toys & treats
to charm the small brown thing to heaven. So light so
dry, so *scritchy scratchy.* What did the poor bird hit so
hard– bloody beak and beady eye– and might it now
be *com-for-ted* on this small bed of fresh green grass?
The mower making four-foot-swaths between the
oaks and giant elms. A clam shell for a kind of pillow,
jacks ball by its head. A scrap of blanket tucks him in.
What I would want, and now I cry for all the people
when I die. I close the lid and tie a string *to keep the*
worms from crawling out, to keep the worms from
crawling in– (a white stone marks its head.

DARLING DEAREST honey boat baby, yummy gorgeous apple brown betty, cozy creamy cutie pie, sweetheart, dovey, sugar lambie, fuzzy bunny lovey dovey, darling pudgie milky mine, won't you be my Valentine? Honey baby bunny dear, *Bumpa, Oompah, Ohma, Dida, Nonny, Popi, Granny, Gramps, Auntie, Nanny, Mamsie, Mommy, Papa, DADDY!* Left his handprint on my fanny. It's not funny– Whack him back! Baby spider snot hole sneak, poopy tattle pervert creep, peasant pinkie pecker-face liar, gross out snot nose rotten stink! Wretched rabies stinking weenie, poophole farthead smooshed banana. *Liar liar pants on fire*, puke hole, stinker, pussy, PIG, pansy, creepo, great big booger– (*know I are but what am you?*

MOONLIGHT LITTERED on the lawn, or is it cherry blossoms all come down. Miniscule grapes in tiny clusters. Vulval cowry held to ear, roar of the waves so far from here. Little white lamb led off to slaughter. Heavenly hosts of blue amber. Breast flesh cut like a flower. *Where oh Where* is my higher power. Come to me now, lie down beside me, as I sleep, toss and turn, dreaming of black men with their cures. Lay it to rest on a board all bound. Whisper the knife, shudder the needle. Suck the feast of the thriving weasel. Purify, and leave me less, but– (*let me be whole.* In my soft sweater, milk's heartbone.

FROM SILENCE to silence– Is that where God lives? In the big emptiness where we are now filled. Follow the screech of a barn owl out– to the wind-crooked pine, a moonless night– I feel as if I am up in the stars, with the fireflies floating on top of the field, all the way down to the road. Rising, Venus shines above, guarding her twin bright stars. When I pick up my cat– she's been following me– her white paws smell of– (*field thyme.*

part two

WHEN THE WINDS CHANGED off the lake– a brisker
blue as the leaves lightened, then clothes thickened to
wool layers and hair got braided. Chestnuts hung in
their spiked burrs. So hard to wait, we sometimes
rattled the limbs instead. Better to let them loosen
alone, each singular, dark-oiled nut within, its light
matte spot like a birthmark. I touched the luscious
red-brown skin over my lips like the perfect kiss, then
hurled it far away as I could– ran to gather a napkin
full, my package of plenty, a rumpy harvest that made
a soft and generous clicking, as they rubbed together,
as I swung my parcel, feeling rich, really loaded.
Autumn releasing her leaves as well. The wind
swirled, making me leap, my lungs grow. I'd rake a
pile to throne myself, count the beads of my chunky
necklace. Brothers hammered a single hole, strung one
chestnut and made it haul. I liked a group of them
together best, like marbles, bagged, or eggs in a nest.
Something about the way they moved– *smooth, dark,
oiled, cool*– (against each other I wanted to know.

FULL-LENGTH, BROWN ZIPPERED iceboating outfits, lined with the curly fleece of lambs, for the Midwest winds that whipped the lake and runners ran– over the ice like thrown knives. Blades flashed, while tears were driven– eyes in the wind like cut glass. I skated away in my sucked mittens, scarf knotted and ankles aching, cheeks rubbed to a bitten shine, the booming voice of a darker depth in the black green thickness of solid ice. It cracked like winter lightning– *struck*, as if it could open and swallow us up. It raced below while I raced above, further and further on the lake's expanse, best when the winter snows held back and the lake was sleek with the piers all in– Wild, like it was when the Indians lived here, had sweat lodges, rolled in snow, the smoky flap and salty leather, bodies of men and women together, dripping away while outside the weather– ripped into all that was human and tender.

FROM THE RAW AIR that claimed March, we ran for the gush in the greenhouse, where peat was heaped and loose to the fingers. Popsicle sticks marked the names of flowers– soft spread of seedlings inching up. The gardener moved in slowest motion, old as the wood that framed this place, with its fragile glass and sprinkler system. Before we knew it– *summer was upon us*, but still we craved the trapped forced heat of the greenhouse. Kreitz gave us butterscotch in twisted wraps, and sometimes we slipped a cigarette from his pack, took it down to the dump to crouch behind tires– this is where the horses were taken when they had to be shot, so we smoked and *fled*, jumping on the back of the battered farm truck, taking the bumps– (*holding onto the pitchfork.*

EASY TO GET SCARED about that ice house– *Oh no, no,* better left unsaid. As if something terrible had gone down there. The perfect place to conceal something awful, like Bluebeard's wives– blood in the sawdust. They used to pack hunks of ice inside here in the heat of the summer. There were no windows, and the doors were thick, eight inches at least, and they bolted shut. Completely dark in the middle of the day, if you were locked in the ice house. You couldn't see a sister or cousin's face, until someone screamed, pounding on the door, yelling bloody murder to– (*Let us out of here!*

LOOKING FOR A PLACE where we could stay separate, watchful, unseen, like down by the lake in the crotch of that willow, surrounded by cedars with their pricker needles. Covered by bushes but close enough to the liquid lap of the foam scum shore to see what was happening, away from the piers and boats that delivered younger sisters and brothers to the screened sandbox and babysitters. We were on the outskirts of law and order, climbing that maple with limbs set perfect– we got so high even we are unnerved, knowing quite well that accidents happened, like climbing that silo after being told not to. *Shall we have ten funs?* Pushing up the lid to the roof on the big house, getting out and leaving him there, forgetting for hours. Scruffed bare knees from the sandpaper tile above the old gymnasium. Usually fine, up high, alert– hiding from someone. Only when we came down to earth did we fight to kill, like that time we camped out over at Auntie's, and nearly murdered each other over a plastic pad of fake butter.

MOTHER COULDN'T STAND our big family dinners, probably because Gramma was at the head of the table, and she served weird food, like sweetbreads, but I liked the commotion and there were slabs of tomatoes we could smother with sugar, pieces of bread, we sliced even thinner, stuffing the inside with marmalade. Mounds of the tiniest, baby bantam corn– we plunged silver prongs and tried to out eat each other. Picture plates worth getting to the bottom. Sliding Sucaryl down Papa's spoon– *swimming swimming swimming*, until it disappeared. "Why don't you take a long walk off a short pier." Hand-painted walls of pheasant in the ferns. One section pounded open with a steel safe behind it. Here it was sunny, unlike Auntie's nextdoor, which was a dark blue-green, but when we ate over there it was never liver and onions. She knew what to serve, though she never had children. Hamburgers, bratwurst, peppermint ice cream. Chocolate soufflés with loads of whipped cream.

BERNARD WAS THE LAST in the long list of chauffeurs. He drove for Little Gramma, who had a grey Packard with a sliding glass panel between the two worlds. We pushed the button down so we could talk to him, and sometimes he'd sing. Bernard lived upstairs in the carriage house apartment. It was creepy and dark. He wanted to be famous. To croon on the radio. Helen and I dropped by as if paying homage, but he drank red wine and I noticed the bottles. Sometimes he seemed too familiar to me, up there in the half-dark with open closets. Helen sort of liked it, but I was more wary, like the time that man approached us with a silver dollar– I turned and ran. I think Helen was pretty tempted by the money, and she wasn't a coward, but at that moment in time, she was my follower. After Bernard left to pursue his career, we'd sneak boyfriends up those abandoned stairs to make out on the sofabed. The place was falling apart with animals in the walls, seedy and hot. They said, Bernard was a failure, a dreamer and a drunk. It can almost make you sad, how lost people get, giving themselves over, like the blood residue in those big gallon bottles.

DRAWN TO EXCITEMENT, not only to dog fights but negative ions, the loser always louder right after some disaster. Ross couldn't stand the fact that I could still get him down, kneel on his shoulders and dangle hair across his mouth. But what I liked most was afternoon thunder, how the sky shifted dark and lit up the color of everything– the sheet of grey water coming across the lake– slamming shut windows, the dust smell of screens, while the oat field by the farmhouse became even more luminous. When the rain hit, face forward, it was like being thrown– I'd run out into the rain and stand under the downspout. They said if we swam, our bodies would get charred. Sometimes at night, we'd watch the crackles of electricity etch the heavens with heat, silent explosions. But I liked it better when it was deafening and wet, strikes coming closer, close to my nature, counting the seconds until the big one fell. In violent downpour. By morning we'd discover which tree had been hit, then walk along the block-long length of it, listening to the men as they sawed the oak into sections, bright smell of wood under the falling pieces.

EVEN THOUGH HELEN was a full year younger, she was a brat when she wanted to be the girls' leader. She got them all to desert my command and join her in the Bunny House. That was their Club, by the compost heap, which took up a serious quarter acre. The Club was real secret and that summer I hated her. Pictures of horses and naked girls tacked up on the walls with a whole set of rules– like where to hide when you were attacked. Cherry bombs exploded with M-80's on the path. The Club reassembled in the gift-wrap room, where they played strip poker, explaining intercourse and the curse all wrong. But I got her back later, when I told the kids on the bus that fall– that her mother wore falsies. My aunt called up and reminded me nicely that a family always has to stick together. Yes, I thought, by ignoring each other.

PADDLING ACROSS THE LAKE to the Pabst Canals, where the slowing swish of seaweed dragged beneath the bow, gondolier style, we pushed on through the greeny mass of water lily pads, trying to be quiet so we could sneak up on creatures. Black-eyed Susan and purple loosestrife grew down to the edge. The bridges were low arching curves of cement. If you sang under there your voice sounded terrific. Sometimes we'd spot a blue heron or a horned owl, super silent, before a turtle plunged or a mallard swam by with her thread of seven. If we got out on one of those islands, we played without sound like Indian children. Life was much better without adults around. We were supposed to wear soggy, thick, orange life-preservers, but we figured it was enough to have them in the boat with us. We were all advanced swimmers, and wouldn't want to tip in those dank canals, because of the muck and bottomless slime. Paddling back out onto open water, it was as if we'd escaped– (*Mother Nature.*

HEATHER WAS THE MOTHER, a gold and white collie, known for saving the life of Georgie when he wandered away from the white picket fence and our Aunt Emily. Bonnie and Bruce were black and white. They had a doghouse with straw inside, painted the same pumpkin yellow as the rest of the place– the loft, the cottage, the old gymnasium, but as far as I knew, not one of them used it after Bonnie had her litter there, twelve all together. Six died immediately during delivery. The other six, wrapped in a woolen blanket, didn't make it either. I arrived just after the event was over, carrying a rubber kewpie doll I'd won at the fair in Okauchee. It squeaked when you squeezed it. Her puppies went silent. The doll was naked and newborn, about their size, lifeless. I went and got the farmer and we buried the lot, back in a place we called the animal graveyard. There was even a horse of Papa's in there. Each animal had a stone, but then it all got grown over. Bonnie stood at the edge and barked and barked, until I gave her my doll to make her feel better. She carried it around in her mouth for months and was the very best mother, though everyone said it was pitiful of her.

THERE WAS A SMALL PATH between our house and
the neighbors. We were usually barefoot and had to
negotiate– even when we reached the soft feathery
grass, it was full of split hickories. There by the path,
were tall hollow reeds we liked to call snake grass–
you could pull them apart, make a necklace or
bracelet. We went over there to build fires on the
shore. Above a teepee of twigs I would cook up our
dinner– crisp, gooey and white– with a bag of marsh-
mallows. Slip the sweet, burnt shell into my mouth
and re-cook the innards. Later we'd catch a jar of
lightning bugs, roll them down the hill. Holding a
couple in my hand I'd watch the lights blink through–
like a flashlight on the palm makes your skin appear
translucent, the mysteries of the flesh were everywhere
around us.

BENEATH THE CARRIAGE HOUSE apartment was a mammoth garage, a cruising arena for swooping brown bats when the sun went down. The carriage stood in the corner under a huge piece of plastic. We yanked it off– and let the brougham shine like a hearse of wet licorice. Up on wood blocks, *off-limits*, they said, but we snuck up anyway, mounting the round metal step. The sumptuous dust smell inside was something like a coffin that's been slept in, then abandoned, stirring up recollections of past incarnations. We pulled the rotting tassels that closed the silk shades. One of the boys was on the driver's seat making the carriage rumble. There was a little round window to look out the rear, with an identical shaped cover, cushioned with black satin– a peephole for lovers– escaping, terrified– we made up the fiction– abandoning all luxury for mother-of-pearl passion. When it got too close, we leapt for fresh air– off the demolished leather, over the oil slicked floor, not knowing the past can crumble even later, like love letters written on crease broken paper.

WE ARE THE MOTHERS for a while. We rock and cook and *coo* and sock and shoe. Gotta stay loose, or forget it. Wish wash, wishy-washy *Dim* dup dribble, take a peek and *Hey* nonny *Hoe* down baby– Sweep let drop, get a legga *Knee* fagabop. Feed a mouth a tabletop and butter on the bedspread, lettuce for a crunch head. Down we go come up and– *Shine!* Gotta struggle to the surface for that blue spank air to pump us full a that good stuff. And it's true a friend can lessen the load. You mixed up with several men, me messed up with mine. But neither of us wants to kiss TV hello/goodbye. I bring you a casserole when you're down with the evening blues, singing your own song– *Long day alone, on the line, in the basket, on the road in the mind.* Felix there is bumped with sleep while– someone wants to– go abandon, someone wants to– Find that partner, dance in the dark like *Goblet spill*– (like goblet spill.

WHEN EVENING FLARES on the cedar barn, I think of the word Toronto, and stick the cold season of experience, for fruit and roses, mingling ripeness. The kinship sound of *Toro*, for there the bull does stand– Stomp in the mind and Dust flies up all around him. *Agh*, this beastly frustration. Damn the dice throw of the stars. And the silvery cabbage plants gone to seed without making one solid cerebrum. And my own brain chugs to a standstill. Yes, I know the fears. If love comes, will it destroy me, in the twenty-seventh summer of my years? No chance, no arrival. The light leaves the cedar barn. (*Why does my face grow suddenly older.*

I'D LIKE TO SEE THE MARRIAGE you imagine possible– Autumn bleeding everywhere, out of the opening in the forest where I'd follow, the trail of your dress to the vows said. Then *bells* of air– *mountains* of air. Vows you have in your texture already taken. Or will you trash it all. Will his doubts un-do? I want you to be happiest, like a parent might– present you with running water for your homemade house, seeing how you're fresh to this union. As crushed pine sends its flavor up, we watch the water crash. Looking down you say, *"This is where he first told me."* I am only a cousin, wanting the best for you, or secretly Greedy commonly typically Wanting you to marry like Me have a baby like Me, so we can be more one in day and expectation. I could ring the copper bowl, write a lyric for the ritual of the first wed evening, but I'm not the man with the words stuck in his thought-box, in the contrary custom, in the cinder stove under the stripped wallpaper, the bare wood the asking. And what if he decides No– what then? And what if he decides Yes. (*What then.*

YESTERDAY YOU BROKE THAT BREAD, left a trail of crumbs behind you. As the jet stream banner falls into little putt-putts friends scatter and are quiet. What sticks in the heart will stay or go enveloped. I sit here, three cups on the desk, one hot one cold one empty, a puff for every line for you, knowing so well in weeks the walls the crib cage of another new apartment. Wondering when the place will be ours alone again, where the fire spoke, crackling the birch, that paper and poems between us. Receiving word of her death in a jolt of newsprint, you slammed against the overstuffed chair, angry, hurt, ridiculed. I went to dip both hands in the lake, hoping to carry away some strength or calmness. Clear wet line across the forehead, cold splashed the cheekbones. Fragments, photos lugged along don't make much difference. You can conjure the people and place for kindling– watch that fire– wait, for the slam that will carry us back to the circle that joins us cheek to cheek hard holding, Cia. August, you say August. Until your notebook bulges, and the baby will tumble in your direction, and you'll die laughing, say– *"Teeth now, Pinko!"* And we'll all rush down to the water. Happy trails across the ocean, until that pilgrimage dead ends, or opens a space– *(neither of us really expected.*

THIRTEEN DAYS WITHOUT YOU, and yet I am not
without you. You are at ease inside me, like a perfect
organ pumping away. I haven't had one jealous thought,
or worried too much about it. You say this week you're
more aware of my absence, like– what to do about
dinner. In retrospect, I'm mildly offended, but realize
how much we do depend, reflect and double each
other's world, nonsense and humor. This lake air is
good for me though, and you've stopped smoking.
More bed to fill, diagonal, but I'm coming to trust, and
think I could even live with myself. No wonder you
miss me, no? I'll thrill to find your searching face, four
hours non-stop from Berkeley. Seven years non-stop,
our brains and bodies nudging each other, and yet I
feel the wings of a future rushing through ozone not
knowing where– til the final explosion slaps one of us
down– Even then, no stopping the beat for the other,
no stopping the changing, altered years.

I KNOW YOU, like nobody knows you, and that is a load. How you twist and thrive on extreme, with the romantic swoon of a home dweller, whiplashed on violence contained, causing your anger. Look out– open the window. It's the quiet hour of the cat. *See*, it drops into the garden. How you want to absorb that singleness, how you want to cry in the movies, and take, as well as be taken. *Oh yes*, and the world must adore you, though your efforts be purely selective your offering small. My God, there is room for improvement. And I don't only mean that the head is too strong for identical, internal likeness, and the hair is impossible. For myself now I'd like to repeat– *No matter what* (expose your flower, let it be touched) *you can go on*. So I say, with the darling hurt heart of a pony, barbed and shaken, that sometimes you can not get out, except to retreat, into the silence that's speaking.

I HAVE PROBABLY WRITTEN you more than any
other person on this earth. It hurts me to think of our
friendship as anything less than immortal. (*Oh, now
I've embarrassed the reader*) but how can I tell them,
that what we have shared, just isn't that common a
thing. We've been on the road with the roof down,
climbed up the hill, scooping up the berries, finding
the righteous, almost, until Otis came on the radio, and
you said, "*Don't cry, you'll be with him, forever now.*"
And I wrote you (quite D. H. Lawrence) that I also
needed a female companion of equal importance in
another sphere. You know, I will always be there for
you, that my lines will continue to travel the distance.
It's an *arc en ciel* that configuration– our pots of gold
spring forth! You are probably the one person in this
world who I will remain at peace with.

TONIGHT I FEEL YOUR ABSENCE. Haunting, echo, hollow. The *whoop* of owls lovemaking surrounds the black oak trees. Reverberation of the moon and her bellow song, if she had one, she'd sing for you, and I can be glad for you, thinking of the breathless doe that will come to your window, and the buck that will press the shape of his sleep in the high grass– *Silence*, that best comforter, when you're comfortable in your own skin, in your north woods trailer, the electric finally in, and no one getting you up at the wrong hour or telling you how to do it. Retiring from these parts that have grown too many cars, too much business. Bad air, bruises. But good things too have grown here, and we have eaten from the hand of your labor. The early morning dew thick hour, the sopping shoes, the cold bent hand that offers. We take. You go– (*like the stars go.*

I WAS TOLD TODAY. Today the trees tolled. Today I went in. Your way today Kate. Today gone to memory. Kate I heard you today. Today I got down. All the trees told me nothing, of what it is not to see today Kate. If I could reach my hand in, under the skin of today, I would stroke the long ribbon of your spine today Kate. I would guard the perimeter of your privacy. I would needle the dark with your talk today Kate. I would moisten the music as noontime rings. All the sandstone doors would swing open today! I would haul in the sky and allow for you Kate. *I was told, I was told.* (I am listening, Kate.

AS YOU SAID, it was short-lived, but does that diminish or heighten it? Sitting here on the window seat, the late afternoon autumnal world is all lit up for a moment. The sky is laden, and the weight of the clouds makes the light appear ravishing, breaking through– waking up the green and the gold of it. The orange-red trees are suddenly luminous as an airy rain falls and I hold my breath thinking– *beautiful, beautiful, beautiful.* Then I look back down to the book I am reading. By the time I glance up, everything is dull. The colors have dropped their radiance. The fields are flat. The sky is sober. The moment of magic for us is over.

MISTLETOE KISS ME STING a waspish. To embrace
the poisoned leaf, white berry bloodless. Poke that
fire started somehow on sheer ice. What melt can do,
what flame say. Snow, well, even covers. Into the long
white dwelling cave we dug our blue. Little bears with
noses *(sniff)* so round our inner heat shone through.
Yet don't forget those freezing tips– even cool bath
water burns it. Hearth can't wait another year. Need
ignition, symbol roaring, right here. Else in cool we
work a bend, to pillar of the past, look back, to stone.
So much gather, sticks fall. Leaves let go. My room
separates from the house, a crack of sky. Now it's time
to knock things back, airtight. Copper plate-back fire-
light for Mood Woman. Call me (wall me) what you
will. *Shhh*, he touches, *nuff now*. Precious heat against
such cave. Conch-song-echo, wing, waves, roll back
to suck the living. Someone younger comes to wonder,
watch and poke and feed the fire. Saw and snap of
small glass ampule, pushing in the luckless sting.
Makes a ring of red in you, a swollen nest, a nauseous
knot. You can not clearly, "Come, wake up." Days

remaindered for a dime. Better sue the cream off that.
Now is time to knock things back. See thick nails
quick up our lean. Tight and squeezed like fancy knees.
By Summit Pass. The height and squeal of car appeal.
We drive into another climb– circling up round Shiver
Lake. It makes us safe inside, in close, where wool and
wheel and cloth slip. Fires blaze along the road. A's
frame the freeze to come, but yellow and red roar now
instead. Hot and cold here meet their net, their duel,
their test. From root to skull, from flower to flow.
Harden, soften, freeze or flame– (*They set a fire in my
name.*

THE LONGEST DAY will drive a crack, til *Jubilate*
windows in. Three parts that braid begin to fly– that
something singing, overlapping. White roses on the
fire lit. The stick once put begins to curl. A wheel is
rolling sparks for ten. She feels it here but far away.
High golden hills remind the day of Saint Johnswort.
One yellow cup upon each end. Tones are gliding
through the light. Mountains can appear we wave–
and roll in dusk and dark til then. Because the small
ones can not stop, we find a way to circle so. We close
into a fire-pop. Open also leaves have room. And
grow with pushes following through. We sing to leap
the last of it. The nuts are gathered in a cup. The arc
is scent, the curve a boat. To row and row the blinding
stream– we hope to cast a shadow yet. A firm trail
makes me follow up. We turn and run descend upon.
To beat a beat upon the rim. A kiss in light before a
name. The same few rise. Until she flew. The angel
woke to be a bird. And never once the same again.
The turquoise turning chamber parts. Lemon mint
upon the flame. Old treasure sack. The tones do

chime. And nut hats six can climb sky high. We wave we wheel around the bend. Though amber's changed the wending way. Sinking deep in Lion's mane. Go round, I say, to sign your flame. Seven stars are shining bright. The round is fine– just out of sight. We see it dry to golden sheets. Though wet was once all flick and stain. Today will not remain again. Go round, I say– go round to me. And let the lifting bird come through. The gate is raised, the sun can too. Go round go round. Today is different yet the same. A new a new. Goodbye in waves for sinking down. Often time to see and bend. Around I say. Once more again. So ashes breathe– (*around me now.*

NOT WHO TO BLAME, not even who do I forgive, just this need to be completely held. To give oneself over, to skin the shining seed– then to bury it. It was a long, slow rain, and it was coming from me, pulled from me, aching, until even the smallest birds bathed in it, and new life came up on its own grief. I will have slept from the birth of light to the death of darkness, and then my time is come to term, this spring. Still, I have these hours, returning to the world, while the rainwater pours, streaming over the roof of this room, and I am deep in my comforter.

part three

SOMETHING IS MET HERE, a strength of will, in a
silent quarry, notch of stone. Almost an absence of air
can you hear it? Up to the peak of a flip-deck fantasy.
A window flies open and something shoots through.
She didn't know *what* she was riding to this, but now
can't get the arrows out. And her little disappointments
are flattering to him, fluttering, *all*, the way he'd look,
in navy, *nice*, a suggestion of biceps. Lying way back
on the saddle– Sky, he catches her hand, she tightens
the pommel. Certain a notion of safety, that nothing
will happen– It's all in her head, until they spot, what?
(*That horse on the loose.*

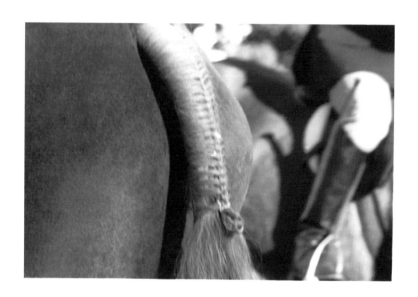

SHE WASN'T A GIRL like other girls were. Something
in her reared and flew. One with the rein and one with
the muscle, holding the hair the impossible hurdle.
Back, far back in our dark soul the white horse prances,
lurking in ancestral genes, Sephardic, in the deep Prime
Woods where her neck snapped, and blood woke, but
she rode again to learn it all– *Uphill fast, downhill slow*.
The softest rattle from across the field, one golden pail
can perk up a ripple for more, *more*. You may feed
your fear in the form of an apple, your lust in the form
of a pear. Place your saddle like a layer of cake upon
another, be gentle with the touch on your reins.
Laughing, her friends, rode the backs of the brood
mares, half-eyed and honeyed with the summer heat,
through the split-melon smell of the mown fields.
And Happy was her name.

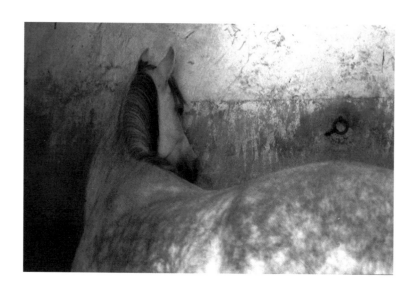

HOW DEEP CAN A COMMENT take you. Suspicious of compliments loading the bed. While the mare knows to leap the ditch like memory, flinch at the click. The hostess can welcome, the dabblers, provide– (We'll write the will, divide the unrequited jewelry, trestle the muscle over an urge to meet.) Forces at work here, *bonnes et bad*. Some people yell at us, "Lawn!" out the window. Some people wave and like us, *shhh*, tip-toe, steel shoe, concentration. You know the mansions. He knows the shacks. I know the houses in between them. Unlikely threesome dressed in language, canter and climb with unschooled grace. How with two fingers to open a horse mouth (with apples). Why it feels better in the dark with the eyes closed. *"Forever, my sweet,"* she turns off the light, slides the rings over, curls into position. Grandmother's linen and the curious quilt of a thousand lives to keep them sleeping soundly.

SHE DREAMT THAT INDIGO was the drug of the gentry. Certain tastes she'd always had. Pick up your courage and walk into the kitchen. This worked, by her upright name. Throw prerequisites all to the wind (in which we're whirling. *Stick with me kid*. Make it burn. He dreamt she was in love with another mood, darker. She dreamt of antlers that stretched across the room. Fresh white birch that looks like chicken meat. Cold breast tastes like chicken-of-the-woods. The mind snaps backwards like a piece of elastic, to the image, words, repeat performance. We'll know when we get there cause we'll all have mouths. That's no preacher, that's a creature! Emptying your pockets of burden in the river. You don't know what it's like to be loving alone.

ONE DOCTOR SAYS THIS, the next contradicts him, the next contradicts *them*, while the excellent maiden hands in her verdict– "*Oh, what the heck.*" It's nice to know someone completely unburdened. Driven to nobody's treeless summit. She won't burst out crying like other women, just hysterical giggles when lowering the box. (Away *away* without a word, to slip off the saddle into a pool of risk. Or is that the ghost horse, Love, in the golden wood, pushing through denseness, for it won't go away, and it lives, though buried, and it speaks to the inner ear like a wishful drum. Most unlikely. But it works its way into her exercise program and Sunday plans. It catches her up in the hair department and widens her waking. Today is: ANYTHING CAN HAPPEN DAY! Areyoureadytodie? Remember my number. Part of her wants to be tiny and free, like and *un*like. Resist, release. (*That horse on the loose approaches.*

HE LIKES TO SEE HER riding in front of him, because it makes him feel younger. *"I'll make him feel younger through the power of my hands."* The battle's between honesty/addiction. The will to deny makes the toothache fonder. Good lost cause. Pelted by light rain the yellow leaves whip to the night slick road. She knows she too could be taken tomorrow, and she begins to think she accepts that, then she realizes, *yes*, that she likes to cry– it makes her expand The Majestic. (Time to get your mind off autumnal obsession– think back to your blonde hair bobbing in front of him, Popi's girl.) He was riding his gelding when it buckled and landed on his first attack. She painted a portrait of that huge brown hunter, wanted to take it to the hospital, but the day it was finished, Mother came to get her and wept before she could mention him.

WHAT SHE'D REALLY LIKE to be is a boy in blue in a tony shirt ad. Make it burn on the best of beaches. Wear no splotch on the kiss of cheekses. Call that crush, One Lucky Guy. *I can't* believe *that you're my friend you're such a jerk!* I love, I love like the waves roll in. Singled out she was to shine. Winship, savor, petrol, pearl– "*Honey, you're a terrific girl.*" Personkind don't measure up, to the mind's meal, the awaited smoke. The feast is held in the mouth of the beholder. Why can't our mornings iron out. How feed harmony, how quell fear? That genius creep that pops out of nowhere, gobbling up specimens, spitting out tractors. She gets real cute to avoid the light. Touching, toughening, tease to cool. Available trouble. Like I, do you? *Come-an, git off yer too high hawse.* (Dreadful, heedless, wonderful choice.

HER RIDING IMPROVED THEIR NIGHT LIFE,
lascivious– that gallop was as good as the best. What
is hard is this body maintenance, this shoeing and
dental and manure business. Hard candy comes to an
end on her breath. He smells the sweetness of apples
in her hair and wonders– What's *she* been up to? As
the days grow darker and the nights, dim, which only
serves to kindle and quicken her fire. The horses
hooves, a tiny banner of blue flames. Suddenly
"looks" are important, and read. (I could take that
jump in your imagination, but bravado I'm trying to
break) since girlhood's confession of lies. Can he fatten
the fortune, yet sleek its sides without paying some
price to the Godhead? Priorities are bid and reneged,
she remembers, when her teenage boyfriend made a
comment about girls who ride want sex. This served
to shock her with denials– "All I want to *do* is kiss!"

SHE RECALLS HER COUSIN with the tug of an accordion, breathing out and breathing in, how the other was the leader in things of danger, how they both felt their bodies change that summer night, hiding in the horse field, full moon, by chance, leaping on bareback– one felt her small breasts bounce and hurt– while the other saw blood by morning. For they were ghost riders, flashing primeval, weightless and high on their invisible saddles, mysteriously right to be riding, forbidden, and the horses too were casting their spells. Years later, by phone– a kind of umbilical– her cousin suggests, *"Ride into the woods!"* They rotate toward smiles as the leaves fall around them, toasted and golden, crushing back into a weightless pile.

AND NOW HAS COME the season of stain. She feels it blaze towards some last chance and tries to catch the meaning fast. The glorious bursts out– Tree Shaped, in dazzling dress, while the small hill on which she stands seems to nearly crumble. Look, there is such mercy above color and grateful water, a body that can *move*, towards an honesty that has to ask for the ability again, to hear it right– What Shines? Behind those leaves that fire and blind us, caught as we are too far, too close– Ah, Great Love can open us. Let us see our lives for what they are, yet nurture a need for kindness, ask that the words come simple and plain, as food after fasting. Delicious to drink in the miracle– Light. Benign, a warmth to wrap her in, before it is time to wake.

THE ANGEL OF THE EQUESTRIANS is with us again this morning, shining through benevolent weather. She has slipped into the quince for a change of dress, that ugly duckling of the apple family. When the horses get a *whiff* of that pungent sweetness, little wings in their mouths start pulsing and we glide. You may not believe in this angel of equestrians, but she moves with us under the tall trees, she leads us through the darkness toward the track. She is beautiful, just beautiful, if only you could hear her laugh, at the mention of "*a death wish to ride with us.*" She knows there is no escape. That the quince will return, even if they're taken, even if you have to wait a year. She sits between the blue reins of the Least Best Bet, leaving all the losers in the dust.

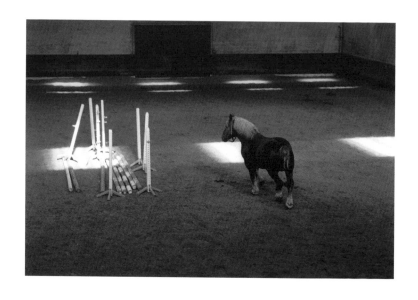

IT WAS SO MAGNIFICENT, they kept *saying*, "Magnificent," with a flourish of hand. The images hammered, like gold but blue, under the perfect canoe ride through a paddle of leaves, and the trees blushed and were spiritually free! Purified, by the one clean blood, she let it go, buried by oblivion, then up, Woke, to the first freeze, where every cosmos hung its head. Scratch of a runner as she bent to squat to make use of nature. Mush, debris, most moist encounter. The lady's ass perceived more perceptively in grey chaps. Generous in mind, in eye, flirtation, cast back, but dumped, finally. She faced an empty glass and plate, scanned the circumference of her self-indulgence. Go break a bridle. For anyone, rightly, most rightly would do. Just slightly burned– (*those hot cross buns.*

MAKE WINTER NICE AND BRIGHT just invite me,
by repeating my name. Repeat without thinking. A
sleigh over snow before any cars come, the incredible
quiet, loaded with soft layers, blankets and horse bells,
her happy face, encircled– his hands, the *shush* of the
runners, oblivious horse flanks, some tender hesitation
til he speaks the truth in deep smooth Italian. Sweet,
sweet cold makes hot the head. "How old are we?"
His hands make her shudder in the carved loveseat,
which tips, knocked over, like a cord of wood– his
yanking the banner to her foolishness. Waking up to
the matches in the hidden niche– "*You asked for it,*"
while the one she imagines, (he will always stand
alone) tips sherry by the mantel in his big black boots.

SHE WATCHED THE BIG MAN make her son scared by putting him up on the unknown animal so that the big man would not feel that fear was beneath him. Who is this gal in cowboy drag, this father pranked with bullwhip? Trotting down the middle of the railroad bridge, fright was a structure to get over with. But did Dad ever crack it? It's best to start so very young that fear's not visible in the field of vision. And yet, it's so exciting. Her penny smothered as the train rolls in– "*When's Daddy coming home?*" Somewhere between these generations falls your Truth or– *Caught you!* Snapshot of baby on her bouncing horse, backward and forward at tremendous speed, with a wooden cylinder through its neck for reins (she would always adore this father) with a hand-painted saddle and silly grin, awfully red, and really raw, almost real, and she rode and rode. But she wasn't allowed to stay down when she got knocked off by that low limb. Even if her sobs refused to stop singing, even if her heart-ring was broke.

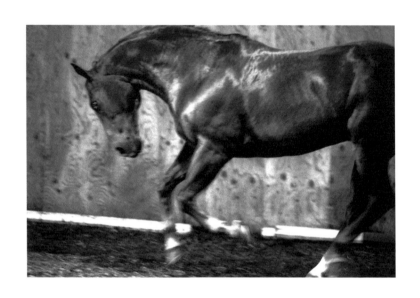

THE PROFOUND BLANKNESS of a deep trance, the crystal's coma would now be nice, as the needle, drill and scalpel scrape– she pictures the power– *unleashed*, through her own gloved hands, the stallion allowed to work and *breathe* up on the top in large green circles, fields alone, the wind released– just to imagine that acceleration, the subtle pressure, leather, response, and liking that, just right between, while the others walked and knew not. She rode– *flew* over pain all bruised and roses swollen, to loosen the bands that clench the teeth, calming down with talk and pat, to await the golden awaited day, when the face is freed like the moon floats over the fields and rounds of hay, the memory filled with the smell of leaves pressed dark with damp and corn fermenting, trees raked, and the air reborn, *renata* to you, who never was even half-afraid by the boot caught trapped in the steel stirrup, the power of all unspoken words, while sighting that trail of glittering sequence, that leads, when followed, to dangerous knowledge.

THE CURVING MOUND was surrounded by mildness. Each smile plunged and came up shining. Oh the laughter rises as the wine descends. (Like, back to Daddy's house, is that it?) For a greater power than she can hold– "*Hold back*," repeats her friend. For just one move could yank the bottom from a pyramid of pains. The face turns downward, shock-like, as her horse collapses to its knees, down in the pasture to scratch its saddle– "*Yeah, but it could of scratched me!*" (Gramma always said the worst accidents happened the last half mile to home.) Galloping over that wide stretch, a thought flashed up– *Everything's so perfect and beautiful, I'd really like to die this way*– but then, pulled back, afraid it would happen. (*Afraid it would never really happen for her.*

METEOR SHOWERS PURGE the Indian summer sky, while boys lie down, sulfur spent, in the middle of midnight cornfields, shorn, to watch for sudden stars. To see some birthday being born. Their mother now remembers well that perfect face of infancy, falling into her fallen arms, pleading with her to re-turn. She hums, she waits for the proper blow to strike her rocking chair with sense. *What knocks?* She isn't a mother like other ones are. But sings as she canters through the wood, baroque tunes that feel of meadow and fox hedges, French horns. No leaves left. And life too dear. Babe in the arms of memory, sears like a shooting star. She should have a blaze on her forehead, to erase her bent– the provocative rip. A modest impulse, high noon. November plainly provides, visibility, (naked, stripped, cold). The heavens too will open and speak in the language of lasting iron and rose.

GREAT BUNCHES OF GIGANTIC gardenia breed and bloom like creatures. She must go to them, their expanding fragrance, for they are at the height of their fullness– voluptuaries of skin. She is drawn to them, shining in the dark, and gathers an armload to her, as if she could press them into her. She would have them transformed into some living gown, and then be born most feminine. But as the flowers fill her hands, she sees that the blooms are melting, and she knows that she has to act now, for the petals are falling, scattered. She would make a deep white bed of them. She would silence the crushing of the hooves. If only this were possible, she would fill his arms completely, as the flowers are filling hers.

THE ONE THAT SHE FEARED all along, horse without rider, that lucky stud, who stalked through the woods and lit up her doorstep, who called but hung up in the middle of the night, his nose is now milky, his muzzle's in her hands, there is nothing to speak of as bliss descends. Here, where the trail stops, she steps out of stirrup and walks into air, this wonder of dream flesh, this ponderous wing. With the stroke of his hoof the fountain is burbling, raising her high above carnal injunction, and she knows, it's the ultimate ride– The End. For a moment, afraid, they'll worry about her, but– How can she part with this superlative, mounting and climbing the staircase to heaven– she never had a laugh so long or good.

HARROW OF A SPLIT/LIFE like blood on the canvas. Watching her own mind, she moves through the interim *thinking about it*. She paces her memory, always thinking about it. Even the breathless extreme of the sauna won't wash, won't clear, what– Can she do. Her passport's expired. Color's hanging in a living basket, but the painter's dead. Oranges taken by a bolt of blue, sliced and maddened like ear from head. If only she could turn it off, not *hear*, the incessant whir of the perpetual picture. Gorgeous green. Tear internal, drawn to ride double, encircle, the chest the loop the neck. Her excited sway upon the high backbone, pulled to the speed of a head-on collision, the inevitable *break-slam*, the bitter bit.

HUSH, WAS WHISPERED, guard it. There is nothing to be done now, listen. Nothing you can do. First snow descends most silent. Falling through worlds to be our covering, our rest, putting us back beside the wood stove, where the copper pot sings for its supper, and the mouths of the children breathe against the frozen glass. There is nothing to accomplish, no test. Just allow that flower to break its sheath of ice, and warming, bloom in brightness. No one has to take it. Nothing to be said. Let it open toward the hills, the higher hills. Let it be the song on which you rise, even as the snow descends, and absence animates the landscape, even at this time of darkness– *sing*, for tomorrow will amaze us, as the constellation rides, and the moonlight doubles in the heart of the beholder, balancing the curving slopes of white.

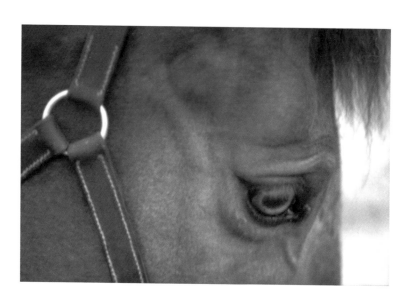

HE DOESN'T WANT TO touch her until goodbye. So
long, Darling, so long held. The old reluctance to let it
go, free fall, into clarity, or– which route? I didn't
even touch our trailing faithful as I drove. Don't ask
where, just leave, *leave*, as I'm leaving you. Perhaps in
this basket, better held empty. For I may break before
I die, break us, break you. Willingly wild, the horses
run forward on the darkening hill, right up to the
moon which dines tonight in fullest form. The orb
diminishing as she climbs. So too, I reach my height
and soar. Off to the big ranch of emptiness now. *"The
sky,"* he said, *"is covered with clouds. Pity,"* he said,
but she thought, No, it makes us feel safer, closer to
earth. She always did want that comforter up, and he
was forever throwing it off. Listen, my love I'll cry
for you. For them. Me too. And maybe then, clouds
all gone, sky blue, clear morning– (*somebody will come.*

THE DANGERS OF DRIFTING while driving in a daze–
loosening the reins that last ride on Eagle. I had the
premonitions that day, galloping alongside Old Farm
Road, newly spread gravel hid the edge of asphalt, my
horse nicked– sliding, weight of horseflesh– *thrown*,
into a splash of view, as if I *were* the landscape, even
liking that later, the wakeful, unexpected, stinging
SMASHEROO. It all felt familiar, as if I'd read that page
somewhere, or someday, like "The End" plucked out of
the saddle, oddly marvelous and shocking, like birth,
but not squeezed, rather– (*Freed* from the tiddlywinks
of shape.

TO SUMMON INSIDE the brave shining warrior, glittering hero of the skies, with flaming sword, astride a horse so white, you *know* you are ready to meet and overpower The Dreadful. I've got my firm together now, my word drawn up, to hold and to swing into warning. Big "L's" begin lifting, for lightness and levity, raising the sediments Up in the body. L is for *Laura* I said with my slipper, for all of the liquid that rises forever and falls into falls, to further the flowing, to keep us in motion. How to walk the white steed, each step lifting and carrying and placing to stand. The electrical smell falls in a ring at your ankles. You *are* the shining rain. You draw a No. 1 in a motion to the sun– The globe itself hovers there before you. Yes, you can touch it, give it a little "L." That's what it's come back for– to set you on your way, gladly, with a hum– (*an approval.*

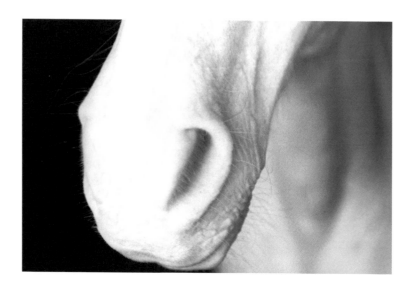

CALL ME WALL me Zucchero. (Catch him if you can.)
Too far gone for halter, lead or lunge line now. A steed
instead, a breed apart, to step or stumble all agog,
ranging on Rose Hill, wandering down the road, a
steady plod before the bridge that he's afraid to cross.
I stand beside you, Zucchero, and watch the waters
gush– the earth is juicy, spilling, rushing from its slit–
the lance that pierced the side of flesh– and out ran
water out ran blood– alive now in this gully– so much
so good to munch. And here I come, your leisure,
with rubber pail and box of sugar, calling you– My
Sweetness– trusting, waiting, listing, leaning, MOON-
less, blotted evening. Grass smell fresh upon his
breath. The taste of brown lump sugar. He lets the
rope go round his neck, loosely leading him along
beside the excavator. He lets me take him over. His
mouth is filled with coated oats, sweetness his last
supper. I kiss him then and taste his tears. His eye is
wide, his head goes up, and suddenly he tumbles. He
stumbles, yet he flies! Bless him now with petals, holy
oil and petals– (*close his open eye.*

I REARED UP AND SAW my matching half, and laughed the laugh God loves when human pain has passed, and the barn doors slide to a warmer state of mind, the kind you get when your man comes home, when you find you're not alone anymore on this hard earth in white December– pipes that froze are running now with water– from another planet, but now he's made it back, following the whinny of the One Sweet Call, which is his name, I say out loud. I rise to meet his face his fur, receive his sure advances, and when he enters through my sleeping hair, we both entwine and laugh the laugh God loves to hear. When we awake, my long long arms wind around him, warm *and* warm. A lovely morning on our dish will come– (*just like the big doors kiss on barns.*

LAURA CHESTER has been writing, editing and publishing since the early seventies. Author of several novels, *Watermark*, *The Stone Baby*, *The Story of the Lake*, and *Kingdom Come*, she has also edited four important anthologies, *Rising Tides*, *Deep Down*, *Cradle & All*, and *The Unmade Bed*. A collection of short stories, *Bitches Ride Alone*, is a personal favorite. Non-fiction works include, *Primagravida*, *Lupus Novice*, and *Holy Personal*, with photographs by Donna DeMari. Chester has two grown sons, and lives with her husband in the Berkshires of Massachusetts. www.laurachester.com/word@laurachester.com

DONNA DEMARI has been shooting fashion since the late seventies. Her work has appeared in many top European and American magazines, including *Vogue*, *Elle*, and *Marie Claire*. DeMari has lived in Milan, London and Paris, and now resides in New York State. Fascinated with the aesthetics of the equine, her horse photographs included here are from a collection of prints, "Flying Mane." ddemari@taconic.net